A LIMITED SEASON

EXTENDED

by
Mark Nicholls

This first edition published in Australia in 2019 by:

Prahran Publishing
P.O. Box 2041, Prahran, Victoria, 3181

© Copyright Mark Nicholls 2019

Mark Nicholls has asserted his legal and moral right under the Copyright Act 1968 to be identified as the author of this work.

Published by arrangement with
Prahran Publishing, Australia.

All rights are strictly reserved.

No part of this publication may be reproduced, stored in a retrieval system or transmitted, in any form or by any other means, without the publisher's prior permission in writing. Copying of this script for performance reasons is also strictly prohibited by law, either in whole or excerpts from.

This book is sold subject to the condition that it shall not, by way of trade or otherwise, be lent, resold, hired out or otherwise circulated without the publisher's prior consent in any form of binding or cover other than that in which it is published and without similar condition, including this condition, being imposed on the subsequent purchaser.

Every reasonable effort has been made to trace copyright holders of material reproduced in this book, but if any have been inadvertently overlooked the publishers would be glad to hear from them. The story, all names, characters, and incidents portrayed in this book are fictitious. No identification with actual persons past or present, places, buildings, and products is intended or should be inferred.

ISBN 978-1-922263-06-3 Paperback
ISBN 978-1-922263-07-0 eBook

Dewey: 822.4

 A catalogue record for this book is available from the National Library of Australia

Performance Licensing and Royalty Payments

Mark Nicholls retains control of both the amateur and professional stage performance rights of this play. No unauthorised performance should occur without the express and written permission of the playwright.

Restriction of Alteration

There shall be no modifications of any kind to the play including deletion of dialogue (including objectionable language), changes to characters gender or names, title of the play or music without the express and written permission from the author.

Sound and Video Recordings

This play may contain stage directions to include the use of music, video or other sound recordings either in part or in whole. The author and the publisher have not sought the right to use such content and performance rights permission should be obtained seperately. Permission to record audio and video recordings of all performances must also be explicitly given by the author in writing.

Author Credit

Performance rights approval requires credit be given to Mark Nicholls as the sole and exclusive author of the play. This obligation applies to the title page of every program or other advertising material distributed in connection to this play. The author's credit should appear immediately under the title of the play on all published material, and alongside no other individual. Font size of credit cannot be less than 50% of the largest letter used in the play's title.

Please email info@prahran.press for all performance enquiries.

DEDICATION

for Joan Lorraine Nicholls (1938-2005) and
Peter Norman Nicholls (1936-1997)

performers, producers, parents

ABOUT THE PLAYWRIGHT

MARK NICHOLLS has been performing on various Melbourne stages since the age of six and has an extensive list of credits as a playwright, composer, singer, actor, producer and director. He is Senior Lecturer in Cinema Studies at the University of Melbourne where he has taught film since 1993.

He is the author of *Lost Objects of Desire: The Performances of Jeremy Irons* (2012), *Scorsese's Men: Melancholia and the Mob* (2004) and recently published articles on Italian Cinema, Powell and Pressburger's *The Red Shoes* and Sergei Diaghilev's celebrated company, The Ballets Russes.

Mark is a film critic and worked for many years on ABC Radio and for *The Age* newspaper, for which he wrote a weekly column between 2007 and 2009.

He lives in Melbourne with his partner, Ali Wirtz, and their two sons Oscar and Carlo.

SERIES PREFACE

I wrote these plays for only one reason, to perform them. I publish them here, therefore, somewhat reluctantly. They were never written to be read on the page by anyone but a treasured posy of performers that I trust to help me rescue them from it. They were certainly never conceived of as works of anything so respectable as literature. Nevertheless, I have found two reasons to overcome my reluctance and my usual roguish prejudice against readers and writers in favour of performers and punters. One reason is that putting these plays into print provides the opportunity for the most engaged of those who saw and heard them to revive and revise the experience. The other reason is archival. I wish to leave a permanent, if inadequate, record of the facts of their production over a decade, in a private space in Melbourne, for the benefit of both a small, dedicated paying audience, and for a smaller band of compulsive show-folk.

Writing these plays for the talented actors, musicians and backstage characters whose creations are recorded here, and having the privilege of working with these artists to produce them, has been the most satisfying occupation of my otherwise horrendously charmed and fascinating life.

Now that they have had their blessed release in print, these plays are beyond the concern of any motivation I had to write them. Read them, o curious one, and work it out for yourself! One motivation I will record, however, rests in the inspiration generously given by those who worked on and attended these cosy performances, and so brought their privileged, fleeting moments of theatre securely into being.

ABOUT THE PLAY

In the early days of, what would become known as, the Ballets Russes, its master and impresario Sergei Diaghilev refused lucrative offers for his company to perform on the London vaudeville stage. Unlike Anna Pavlova, among others, Diaghilev had no wish to compete with the stage jugglers, fire eaters and performing elephants that would inevitably crowd his dancers for the sort of attention he believed they deserved. He relaxed this prejudice in later years – maturity often allows us to lower the bar – but for a Gilbert and Sullivan man, his professional attitude in those early days seems surprisingly precious. Diaghilev chanced his luck with a horse on the opening night of *The Firebird* in Paris in June 1910. But that *was* Paris, and the first night gift for the company that the horse left on the stage floor probably sealed the fate of all animals working with the Ballets Russes until well after all moral and aesthetic barriers came down with the catastrophe of the 1914-18 war.

A Limited Season (Extended) began life as *A Limited Season*, the equivalent of an elephant act, in a double bill following the short play, *Richard The Second and the Old Queen*. The first half of the bill had Madeleine Swain playing a mad and lovesick Elizabeth I, thinking she was Richard II and running around her palace late at night reciting the best bits of Shakespeare's poetical drama. *A Limited Season* was therefore intended as a three-scene joke to lighten the mood of the evening after the serious business of Madeleine's work of emotional hari-kari. It was only with its eventual extension that we had the leisure to say something more about the accidental nature of this 'dynamic duo', the protracted farce and the great deal of fun that comes with all such enduring partnerships.

My parents, Joan and Peter, weren't like their fictional namesakes at all. Neither of them ever taught at a university, played a season at the Tivoli, or lived long enough to find themselves confined to a retirement village or sunset home. If they did indulge in recreational drug use or pathetic, narcissistic infidelity, they had the good sense to keep these human weaknesses from their children. What they didn't hide from us was the incessant banter of married life. Nor were we spared a degree of exposure to the showfolk rough and tumble of teaching in schools, performing music and fighting with their, no doubt somewhat bemused, educational and ecclesiastical backers.

My parents certainly had an advanced capacity for endless bickering and argument, but I honestly can't remember any of the causes of discord. My fondest memories of them are when they were drinking sherry and planning the next concert or talking over some new idea for running one of their choirs.

The Peter and Joan of this play have only brief moments of such charm, but they do have that extreme thirst for the next show that my Peter and Joan would have undoubtedly maintained had they hung around to play the extended gig that is the sunset circuit.

CHARACTERS

PETER: an actor of eighty-five who acts like he is fifty. From Act Two he is forty-five.

JOAN: an actor of eighty-five who wishes she were fifty but acts her age. Later she too is forty-five.

HARRIET: an aged care facility worker who, at thirty-five, is happy as she is.

AUDREY: a dental hygienist in love, also thirty-five.

IAN: a wealthy solicitor of thirty, also in love.

OSCAR: a stage manager of seventeen, briefly intoxicated.

A Limited Season Extended was first performed at Rear 4, Clifton Hill, Victoria on the 20th of May 2015 with the following cast:

Joan: Madeleine Swain

Harriet: Caerwen Martin

Peter: Mark Nicholls

Audrey: Caerwen Martin

Ian: Luke Van Ryn

Oscar:	Oscar Wirtz
Director:	Mark Nicholls
Lighting Designer:	Oscar Wirtz
Assistant Stage Manager:	Carlo Nicholls
Co Producer:	Alison Wirtz

Act One was produced as *A Limited Season* and first performed as the second half of a Double Bill with *Richard the Second and the Old Queen* at Rear 4, Clifton Hill, Victoria on the 1st of March 2012 with the following cast:

Joan:	Madeleine Swain
Harriet:	Grace Taylor
Peter:	Mark Nicholls
Director:	Mark Nicholls
Co Producer:	Alison Wirtz

ACT I
SCENE ONE:

As the lights come up and the music fades we see JOAN and PETER sitting at a table, as if in a restaurant, waiting. The table is set with a small white vase of flowers, wine glasses, knives and forks.

PETER: I don't really see why we have to meet this girl for lunch at such an ungodly hour of the morning. Don't these kids know anything? For God's sake, we did a show last night!

JOAN: It's half past one, darling. And it was a lunchtime matinee for old age pensioners, and it was over by two. The afternoon tea was finished by four.

PETER: Two hours of tea and passionfruit sponge and not a drink in sight.

JOAN: Exactly. Hardly a riotous, all night orgy! You were tucked up in bed by ten.

PETER: Still, I must say, her letter was uncommonly courteous.

JOAN: I'm impressed she actually sent a letter. From what I understand, it seems that anyone under thirty that wants to get your attention these days simply announces it on Facebook.

PETER: *[He knows full well.]* What on earth is Facebook?

JOAN: Start walking at electric light, take a line through the telephone and telex, keep going and you will get there eventually.

PETER: Oh my God, it's like that 'email' thing all over again.

JOAN: They do say the web is a useful way to find work – especially in film.

PETER: Yeah well when they find a way to let casting directors check out the size of someone's tits and arse on-line, I'll consider it.

JOAN: I think someone in a related industry has already worked that one out, my love. Anyway, this young woman seems very thoughtful.

PETER: Yes. I was impressed that she even managed to remember my correct title.

JOAN: I thought you would like that. That Honorary Doctorate in Music Theatre has paid for itself over and over again.

PETER: It wasn't Music Theatre it was Cultural Studies. And I didn't pay for it, if that is what you are implying. It was awarded to me for my services to the discipline.

Act I – Scene 1

JOAN: Cultural Studies? I can't see how. You never did an ounce of study that I ever saw and neither 'culture' nor 'discipline' are words that immediately come to mind when I think of you.

PETER: It was a great mistake that they gave you a diploma for your two years at that drama school. It produced in you an advanced state of pretension.

JOAN: It was a Bachelor's degree in Fine Arts actually.

PETER: Bachelor of Fine Arts, my arse! From all I heard from Barry, when he taught there, you lot spent most of your time with your legs in the air.

JOAN: That is extremely vulgar! Not to mention untrue. If my legs ever happened to be in the air it was probably during some exercise designed to produce deep concentration. All part of a little theatrical innovation that seems to have passed you by – it's called the Method.

PETER: Deep concentration. More like deep penetration.

JOAN: Will you shut up! You are obviously nervous. For Heaven's sake, I've never seen someone get so worked up over a little lunch meeting with a child.

PETER: I'm not nervous. Anyway, this is hardly the first time I've had lunch in here with an attractive younger woman.

JOAN: Right. You are talking about Penny Lambert now, are you?

PETER: Yes. I wondered if you knew about that.

JOAN: Of course I do. She came running to me in tears, straight from the restaurant, apologising profusely for not wanting to sleep with you.

PETER: Oh really?

JOAN: She said she didn't think it was good for her professional development.

PETER: And I suppose you agreed with her?

JOAN: Not at all. In fact I told her that I thought being taken to lunch, talked at, screwed and then never spoken to again was about as accurate a professional development experience that I could imagine.

PETER: You have an unbelievable capacity to reduce something beautiful and romantic to something that is incredibly crude.

JOAN: And you have an unbelievable capacity to misread childish flattery as sexual arousal. But you can forget about that in this case. *[Points to the letter]*. And how do you know she's attractive anyway? More to the point, why do you think she would be attracted to you? This isn't flattery. This is a very considered and thoughtful letter. She has obviously done some research on us – her grandparents probably gave her the idea – and she's come up with a very good idea for

Act I – Scene 1

a show, and she wants us. If you are going to bugger it up by turning it into yet another old man fantasy thing it's too much.

PETER: All right, you've made your point.

End scene.

ACT I
SCENE TWO:

As before. The table setting has been changed. The wine glasses have been replaced by water glasses, the knives and forks for spoons.

PETER: *[Pacing.]* Well where is this woman? She's late.

JOAN: She's not late. We just got here twenty minutes early – as usual. To be honest I don't know what has come over you lately. All your life you've been late for casting calls, late for rehearsals – Good Lord, your performance style could well be described as one missed cue after another. All of a sudden you hit maturity and you can't wait to be early.

PETER: I'm getting slower and I don't want to miss anything. I don't know. Perhaps I'm edgy.

JOAN: What on Earth have you got to be edgy about?

PETER: Well, I don't know about all this. We don't know anything about this girl. It's not going to be another one of these brainy, tours de force things is it? Incessant philosophising and endless bloody warm-ups.

JOAN: Well it wouldn't hurt you to brain up a bit more in your work. Some more rigorous warm-ups wouldn't hurt you either. In that

	football docudrama we did last year, you were the fattest, most unfit and least researched Ron Barrassi I ever saw.

PETER: I once worked with on old guy who refused point blank to do any warm-ups. He said, "Frankly, my dear boy, I've never understood this modern mania for 'warm-ups'. In my day a 'warm-up' was a strong cup of coffee, a cigarette and a fleeting glance at the front page of *The Age* newspaper!"

JOAN: Yes, well I'm pretty sure you modelled your stage persona on that old fella. You put on a big queer voice, pretend to be about ten pounds heavier than you are and, therefore, always get out of doing anything in the least bit physical.

PETER: Oh really? Well it's certainly a long time since we've seen you whipping off your kit and dashing about the stage in paroxysms of physical pleasure.

JOAN: I leave that to Chunky Move.

PETER: Darling, that's exactly what the reviewers called it in that film musical when we had to do the "twisting by the pool" routine.

JOAN: Yes 'Funky Granny' and 'Groovy Grandpa'. Don't remind me.

PETER: Well, if we end up doing anything with this child, I am going to insist on invoking the 'Under 40' rule about dancing.

Act I – Scene 2

JOAN: And that is?

PETER: *[As if reciting a contractual clause.]* "No dancing with or in the presence of person or persons under the age of forty, not excluding crew, audience and front of house staff." I want it in the contract.

JOAN: I am sure that clause we be greeted with general relief. What about nudity?

PETER: Oh for goodness sake! We've been letting that one go under the "let the buyer beware" section for years.

JOAN: That's true. If anyone wants to see me starkers, that's their lookout. I'm long since caring about that one.

PETER: Well, that's not strictly true. What about that show we did in Waurn Ponds when your old boyfriend turned up?

JOAN: You are still bubbling with jealousy about that one, aren't you? And it wasn't Waurn Ponds, it was Moonee Ponds.

PETER: Well wherever it was, you are the one that made such a fuss about it.

JOAN: Only because when he dumped me he became a vicar and developed a heart condition.

PETER: In that order?

JOAN: What news of dear Audrey?

PETER: I don't see what my wife has to do with it.

JOAN: It's just that we haven't heard from her in a while. You can always tell when business is bad.

PETER: That is completely unfair and, I might add, unworthy of you. As far as I know, she's leading a perfectly respectable life with a man who owns, what I believe, is a highly profitable pool and spa cleaning initiative.

JOAN: Still keeping her eye in in the dental hygiene line, is she?

PETER: I gather pool and spa purification has made dental hygiene somewhat superfluous. Anyway you ought to be grateful to 'dear Audrey', she's a good sport. For a civilian she's always been very reasonable about you, when she could have been quite nasty.

JOAN: I suppose that is true. It can't be particularly helpful to a respectable woman's moral fibre to burst in on a dress rehearsal and find me with her husband in a comparative state of undress.

PETER: That wasn't a dress rehearsal, it was your dressing room.

JOAN: But we did have to do it on stage in that one, didn't we?

PETER: Yes unfortunately.

Act I – Scene 2

JOAN: I don't know why you say unfortunately. That was probably the best sex we ever had.

PETER: It's quite disturbing how you can only manage to reach orgasm when there are at least a hundred people watching. Is that why we never play at La Mama?

JOAN: Or that shabby little Rear 4 place in Clifton Hill! No, I don't really have any problem there. I just never bother with all the stage business when we are doing it for real. Best to save it for the paying customers.

PETER: I think Audrey's problem was that when she walked in on us we sounded as if we were playing to a capacity crowd.

JOAN: No. I think it probably went back further than that to when she first met you. Her main problem was that she didn't know what hit her. She never really saw you coming.

PETER: Well, she did as a matter of fact.

JOAN: What do you mean? *[Realising.]* Oh yes that's right. What I believe is described in your bio as "a brief but not uninformative stint in the adult film industry".

PETER: Yeah. Except I usually shorten it to 'the AFI'. It maintains a certain respectful ambiguity. It works in America too.

JOAN: It's amazing how many legitimate actors managed to get a leg-up in the AFI.

PETER: Up and over, darling.

JOAN: Of course. *[Now disapproving.]* Absolutely disgusting.

PETER: Well, at least it was steady work and far more respectable than that university gig.

End scene.

ACT I
SCENE THREE:

As before. The water glasses have been replaced by plastic child cups with lids and plastic straws.

JOAN: Why did you take that academic job, anyway?

PETER: Because I couldn't get any decent work as a cruise-ship crooner.

JOAN: Berlusconi beat you again, eh? There must have been something good about it. You stayed in it for long enough.

PETER: They pay was good and the conditions were tolerable, but after the Dawkins Review all the fun went out of it. The place filled up with all these swatty little academic types who seemed to take umbrage at the tried and tested idea that a lecture is basically just a stand-up comedy routine.

JOAN: Yes. An extended season, reasonably good houses and plenty of opportunity to try out new gags.

PETER: Yeah not so reasonable houses after that internet thing came in.

JOAN: Ah, the filthy little spectre of 'E teaching' and 'distance learning'.

PETER: Yes, terrible sound quality, one fixed camera and no qualified director. All to bridge the tyranny of distance between Parkville and East Malvern.

JOAN: That was the end of a lot of good performers.

PETER: Almost as bad as the Talkies!

JOAN: Video killed the radio star!

PETER: I suppose, when you think about it, most of us were pretty much left over from the silent era.

JOAN: Yes, but at least they knew how to take a cue. From what I could gather, the lot that came on at uni after you seemed to have problems reading the signs. Trying to chat to people at that last book launch we went to was like an endless parade of monologues in search of some connecting dialogue.

PETER: Academics don't chat, my love, they 'discourse'. I tell you out there it's a case of narcissism one, empathy nil.

JOAN: You had a lucky escape. It was lucky Emily came along when she did and was able to spice up your package a bit.

PETER: I'm not quite sure that's such a wise choice of words, dear. Anyway, I would be quite happy still working there if I thought there was any chance your daughter would give up that tarted-up little talent agency and go back into the theatre again.

Act I – Scene 3

JOAN: Our daughter, Peter. Try to remember! And it's not a tarted-up little talent agency; it's a head-hunting company – Executive Human Resource Procurement Australasia. But come to think of it, that does sound a little like some sort of high-class pimping service, doesn't it?

PETER: It's certainly not a decent way to make a living.

JOAN: Well, you can hardly call what we did any better. 'Make a living?' A 'living' is what the Church of England dishes out to miserable country vicars in PG Wodehouse novels – the rest of the scraps of society get served up to us actors. Emily was hardly going to make anything like a living in our business. I think HR was a really good move for her. She's got a lot of responsibility and, from what I gather, she makes an absolutely astronomical salary.

PETER: Blood money.

JOAN: Well, you hardly had any better ideas for her. When she left uni and had huge debts, you seemed to be suggesting she finance them by going on the game!

PETER: Well, at least that's a dignified occupation, with a sense of tradition. *[Looking at his watch.]* Look, now she is late. Can't we order a drink? If I don't get at least three Manhattans into me before two-thirty, I'm a wreck.

JOAN: Ah, the Wednesday Matinee routine. I remember it well.

PETER: There's no need for you to be so self-righteous. I seem to remember you resorting to one or two little pharmaceutical comforts to get you started over the years.

JOAN: Arriving at the theatre with one or two vitamin pills under my belt, hardly compares to you stumbling on stage primed with paint-stripper.

PETER: Vitamin pills topped off with a pseudoephedrine chaser! Or so read the toxicology reports from at least one of your numerous stomach-pump episodes.

JOAN: Honestly, Peter. Anyway, shut up, I think this is her.

PETER: Do you think? Actually, she looks familiar.

JOAN: She does. In fact, I am sure I have seen her before.

PETER: She looks like that kid who always played the Naughty Nurse in the old AFI days.

JOAN: Which right about now would make her exactly seventy.

PETER: She does look very familiar, though. You don't think she's been stalking our shows to see if we're any good, do you?

JOAN: Since when did you ever take any notice of anyone in the audience? With your eyesight you would be struggling to see past Row C anyway.

Act I – Scene 3

PETER: She's very casually dressed for in here. It's a wonder Pierre let her past the front desk.

JOAN: With that body she can get away with wearing anything. Do you think we can sneak away? She looks far too intimidating.

PETER: Look out she's seen us. Oh God, she's coming over.

JOAN: Goodness, she looks like she's running towards us at a million miles an hour. You don't think she's on speed, do you?

PETER: You're the expert. How's my hair looking?

JOAN: What there is of it is holding up admirably. I'd advise you to check your fly, however. That's usually the problem.

HARRIET bundles in pulling up her sleeves to get to work.

HARRIET: Here's my favourite girl Joanie. Chatting to your boyfriend again are you? G'day Pete. Can't keep you away from her, can we? *[They are bemused and speechless.]* Well I'm afraid I'm going to have to break up the party dears. *[She speaks louder.]* Time to be getting on. It's three o'clock, not long before you have your tea. Joanie, we're due for our nice bath, and Pete, Brian's waiting for us to help us on and off the toot. All right? *[She leads JOAN off.]* Yes. We'll like that won't we – bit of a relief after all the excitement.

PETER looks astounded.

End scene.

ACT II
SCENE ONE:

A theatre dressing room. Forty years earlier. There is a two-seater couch upstage centre, a long bench downstage centre with two chairs and places set for actors' make-up and mirrors. Clothes horses and things hanging and some flowers are about the room. The dressing space is implied just offstage. As the lights fade up PETER rushes on, still changing, and heads for the make-up. We can hear JOAN changing just outside stage left.

PETER: *[Entering]* You'd better hurry up. We've only got a minute.

JOAN: *[Off]* That's the last time I agree to do a geriatric bit. I'm far too young for it.

PETER: You said that twenty years ago.

JOAN: *[Off]* Yes, well that was almost exactly at the point when they put that bit into the show.

PETER: When I put it into the show.

JOAN: *[Off]* Yes that's right. How could I forget? And you pinched it from your grandfather and all.

PETER: There's no need to be nasty about my grandfather.

JOAN: *[Entering]* I'm not. He was brilliant; and he did that bit marvellously at the old Regent Music Hall in nineteen hundred and seven; and it was funny. It was ironic when we did it twenty years ago at the Tivoli; and it was still funny. Now it's just sad.

PETER: There's nothing wrong with it at all. It's just entering its rococo phase. Besides, this is review. It's supposed to be old, ironic and sad.

JOAN: Yes. Exactly like its audience.

PETER: Yes, well you just get busy with the war paint, darling. We've only got about thirty seconds and you've got to lose at least twenty years to be convincing for the Ipanema bit.

JOAN: Don't worry about my make-up. You just concentrate on your chord changes and your Portuguesh. I heard they had that lot from Sao Paolo out front last week, and when the boss asked one of them how he liked the song, he said he didn't really know it, but he was sure the Czechoslovakian Football Association were very happy with it as a possible anthem for the next World Cup.

PETER: The next World Cup is not in Czechoslovakia, it's in West Germany.

JOAN: Yes, well that's a pretty good indication of what the Communist Party think of your Portuguese pronunciation.

PETER: Oh, shut up.

Act II – Scene 1

JOAN: Speaking of out front. Did you see Audrey and Ian out there?

PETER: No. I don't think so. Why?

JOAN: Oh no reason. I just expected them to meet us here, that's all. We are supposed to be going to Leo's later, aren't we?

PETER: I think so. They'll probably be here when we get back. Unless they have finally had enough and abandoned us.

JOAN: Enough of the show?

PETER: Enough of us! I'm pretty sure they had enough of the show, poor darlings, about five minutes after it opened in March 1950.

JOAN: No. Ian said the other day that he thought it was still going pretty strong well into the Olympiad.

PETER: Rome or Tokyo?

JOAN: Melbourne, darling.

STAGE MANAGER: *[Off]* Come on you two.

PETER: Right-o.

JOAN: And remember, Peter, it's supposed to be about ;The Girl from Ipanema', not the busty blonde in the third row!

PETER: What ever happened to 'the customer's always right'?

They rush off and we hear a door slam. The stage remains empty for a while. Then we hear the door reopen and Audrey enters, looks about and settles nervously on the couch. She tries to read a magazine but cannnot concentrate. After a while Ian enters.

IAN: Ah. You're here.

AUDREY: I just arrived.

IAN: Did you see them?

AUDREY: No, they were off into the next bit before I got here.

IAN: What are they up to?

AUDREY: 'The Girl from Ipanema'.

IAN: Hell, that's awful.

AUDREY: *[Snapping]* There's no reason to be unkind.

IAN: What?

AUDREY: Well, I seem to remember you thinking it was pretty good.

IAN: Yeah, for about the first five years.

AUDREY: So, you should be long past complaining about it now.

IAN: What's the matter?

Act II – Scene 1

AUDREY: You know perfectly well what's the matter.

IAN: Of course I do. I'm sorry.

AUDREY: No, I'm snapping. I'm sorry.

IAN: I love you.

AUDREY: I love you.

A pause.

IAN: I'm glad we missed them. They are always so *[looking for the word]* vituperative before that part of the show. One of them was bound to snap at us and then I would have lost my temper and just let them have it there and then.

AUDREY: Like that time in Sydney when she threw that script at you and you covered her in talcum powder. Just before she had to walk on.

IAN: She was supposed to be playing Juliet and she went on for the love scene looking more like Miss Haversham.

AUDREY: Well, she was far too old for Juliet.

IAN: She was always too old for Juliet.

AUDREY: Well how can you expect a woman of twenty-two to be really convincing as Juliet when she lost her virginity at seven and a half.

| IAN: | Don't be ridiculous, she wasn't seven and a half. She was at least fifteen – and 'lost' is hardly the expression I would use. |

AUDREY: What expression would you use?

IAN: Well, given that it was with a ninety-two-year-old casting agent, I assume the tax department would suggest it falls under the category of 'Business Expenditure'.

AUDREY: I never really believed that story, you know. I think she was probably twenty-one and she did it with a pimply and sentimental boy by the seaside. She was always a hopeless romantic, however hard she tried to pretend she wasn't.

IAN: Well, if that's true, it wasn't by the seaside it was at the snow. And my pimples were well gone by then.

AUDREY: Do you miss that girl?

IAN: Sometimes. But then I think of you and I don't.

AUDREY: I love you.

IAN: I love you.

AUDREY: Big Sigh! I'm glad we've got a few minutes alone together before we tell them. It's only a few hours since we were all at breakfast, but it seems like ages.

IAN: I know. And after we tell them we can begin our life all over again in peace and quiet.

AUDREY: Not too quiet I hope.

IAN: That's not what I mean. Besides I have booked a little place, miles away from anyone, so we can roll around on that bed and scream our heads off to our hearts' content.

AUDREY: It's a rare collaboration. *[Thinking a second.]* Is that really what you like to do?

IAN: I honestly don't know. After sleeping with Joan all these years I have never been able to get a word in. Though at least her vocalisation stops me from nodding off.

AUDREY: Peter gets so wrapped up in his own dirty-talk that I'm sure he hardly knows I'm there at all.

IAN: You're not going to miss that?

AUDREY: You're sure you are going to be able to stay awake?

IAN: OK. I'll stop. But I am a little self-conscious at being fully naked in front of you. I don't even own a pair of pyjamas. We've known each other for so long. We know so much about each other.

AUDREY: I know what you mean. When you've bared your soul to someone already, there's always the chance that eventually baring your breasts is going to be a bit of a letdown.

IAN: Exactly. It's much easier to get naked with someone you hardly know. It evens up the stakes.

AUDREY: Perhaps that's why we agreed to wait? Put it off until there's no chance of turning back?

IAN: Not at all. We agreed to wait so we could have a clean conscience when we told them.

AUDREY: Not all that clean, my love. What about that time at that Logies party?

IAN: *[Pointing his finger.]* That was not sexual relations.

AUDREY: Well, whatever it wasn't, it was all over my dress. And I didn't know it was there until I went out into the sunshine. Had a hell of a time explaining it to the dry cleaners.

IAN: But they got it off?

AUDREY: No, I decided to keep it for posterity.

IAN: Not really?

AUDREY: Of course not.

IAN: Someone's going to do that one day and cause a lot of trouble.

AUDREY: Well, I don't need to. I don't need any souvenirs. I know what really happened and it was wonderful.

Act II – Scene 1

IAN: Besides, everyone knows what happens at the Logies stays at the Logies. And it's really only been two or three times since we knew how we felt about each other.

AUDREY: And a couple of times before that.

IAN: Is that the way it was for you?

AUDREY: Not really. But you never really know how you feel about someone when it's all starting. Perhaps we still don't know?

IAN: We have time to find out.

AUDREY: We do.

A pause.

IAN: What the hell! Why don't we just tell them when they get back here and get the thing over and done with?

AUDREY: No, I think we should do as we planned. Let's get out of here and get them into Leo's. When I told Alfredo what was happening he gave me a table in the middle, not a booth, and the whole place will be full of thesps, so once we tell them there will be no chance of any really convincing dramatics.

IAN: Yeah that's good. He's a great guy, Alfredo. Also Larry's in town doing that Shakespeare film. He's bound to be there, so there will be no chance at all that anything Joan and Peter can try on will pass muster.

AUDREY: Exactly. But I am not really worried about how they are going to react. It's what they are going to think that disturbs me.

IAN: Who knows what actors ever think? Do they ever think? It's all reaction and show as far as I can see.

AUDREY: They're bound to think about this, surely?

IAN: I doubt it. When was the last time you ever had the sense that Peter was really thinking about anything other than his hair?

AUDREY: I'm pretty sure they think when they're on stage.

IAN: Well, I'm not sure of that at all. I think they're just programmed into a mechanised sort of stupor, and they turn on when someone says 'three minutes' and turn off when someone else says, 'Darling, it was marvellous'.

AUDREY: I'm afraid Peter's going to be really furious.

IAN: I don't see how he can be. We've done nothing wrong. Well, not much at least. We can't help it if, after years of abuse, neglect and a fair bit of casual rudeness, we have found solace in each other and fallen in love.

AUDREY: So do you think that is all it is?

IAN: No I don't actually. But as far as they are concerned, it's enough to get started with. If he tries any rough stuff, or if she tries any

Act II – Scene 1

waterworks for that matter, they will be acting like complete hypocrites and I will have absolutely no respect for either of them.

AUDREY: I didn't think you did anyway.

IAN: Well, not much.

AUDREY: You know, I've wondered if they will be secretly quite happy about it all.

IAN: What do you mean?

AUDREY: Well, they can't have been very happy all these years. Their careers seem to have gone downhill since the day we married them. It can hardly have been much fun with us moping around them all this time. I sometimes think they might have been happier playing the party scene, or even just left to themselves.

IAN: What, do you think they're on together?

AUDREY: It's possible. I have often wondered whether we might walk in on them one day and find something we absolutely do not require.

IAN: Or do require, when you think about it.

AUDREY: But then again, I suppose I think of them as such an old married couple that the inclination to have sex is probably well passed.

IAN: It might be a bit early for that. It's probably more the fact that they are so narcissistic that even going to bed with each other is a bit of an interpersonal stretch.

AUDREY: Then again, this could all just be wishful thinking on our part. It would make it a lot easier for us if we did find that they had been lying to us all these years. But I doubt it will turn out that way. My guess is that they are so wound up in themselves and what they are doing that they have no thought of anything else, that they have no idea that we love each other and that when we tell them we're leaving together they will probably be totally devastated.

IAN: Maybe. So why don't we just leave them a note? We're not actors. We don't need a scene. After all we've been through with them, what do we really owe them?

AUDREY: That's exactly it. After all we have been through with them, I think we owe them quite a lot. We have got to face them.

IAN: I don't care about them anymore. I think we own much more to each other. We're in love. If they can't understand that, it simply proves our point. But I will go through with it, if you want.

AUDREY: We don't have much choice now. It's coming to an end and they'll be here in a minute.

IAN: What about the encores? They should give us a minute or two.

AUDREY: Forget it. They petered out years ago.

End act.

ENTR'ACTE:

PETER is on stage playing his guitar and trying to look really cool wearing black clothes and sunglasses and singing 'The Girl from Ipanema' in Portuguese. Once he has finished JOAN enters as his exasperated wife and the mother of his children with little time for his antics. She sends up his embarrassing attempts at being cool by singing the song in English and in doing so emphasising that the eponymous girl may well have an unpleasant personal odour ("when she passes, each one she passes goes ugh") and anyway, has no interest in him, looking "straight ahead not at he".

End entr'acte.

ACT III
SCENE ONE:

A theatre dressing room as before. It is the next morning. The room is as it was the previous evening except that the rubbish of champagne bottles and other riotous party effects are scattered about. When the lights come up, we see a dishevelled stage manager asleep on the couch. After a while we hear the door open and close and AUDREY and IAN enter. AUDREY goes over to the stage manager to wake him.

AUDREY: Oscar. Oscar. Wake up.

STAGE MANAGER: What? What's happening?

IAN: Are you all right, Oscar?

STAGE MANAGER: Frankly no.

He looks about calmly then bolts to the door as if about to vomit. From what we can hear, he does so.

AUDREY: That poor boy. Do you think they got him drunk? What on earth has been going on here?

IAN: Looks like the crew raided the fridge.

AUDREY: I doubt it. Peter keeps that key pretty tight.

IAN: Oh well, they're obviously not here.

AUDREY: Yes, but where are they? We were at Leo's for at least three hours and they weren't at any of the other places. And how the hell did we miss them between the stage and here in the first place?

IAN: There's obviously a secret door and they never told us about it. They probably put it in for The Beatles.

AUDREY: Well, they've never used it before. I'm getting worried.

IAN: Who knows? Maybe they've anticipated us and got in first.

AUDREY: Well, they had better be in hospital or something really bad, because if I find they've just been avoiding us I'm going to kill them.

IAN: Well, they've done that before. I'm sure they're fine. They've just gone on a bender and, as usual, forgotten all about us.

AUDREY: Do you think so?

IAN: I'm almost certain.

AUDREY: Well, this is really the last straw. *[She sits at the dressing table and writes.]* You are right. We are not actors and we don't need a scene. I'm going to leave this note and then let's head off to Spencer Street. Our life starts on the 11.30 train.

Act III – Scene 1

> *AUDREY shows him the note but the audience cannot see it. She places the note, upside down on the dressing table. She then gets up and heads straight into IAN's arms.*

IAN: Good. And you're totally sure?

AUDREY: Completely sure. They gave us our freedom when they ducked out via the Fab Four escape hatch.

IAN: Whereas we have more dignity. We can leave via the stage door.

AUDREY: Clearing a path between the backstage crazies and the autograph hunters as we go.

IAN: I am so relaxed I may even pause to sign one or two, 'The Former Mr Joan Moet'.

AUDREY: 'The Future Mr Audrey Norman'.

IAN: Hang on, that's not right. I'm not about to take Peter's name.

AUDREY: Well, you changed yours for Joan.

IAN: Good God! Do you know, after all these years, I don't even know your maiden name.

AUDREY: That's all right. I don't know yours either.

IAN: Don't you remember? It's Sutherland. She made me change it because she didn't think 'the Australian theatre' had room for two Dames Joan.

AUDREY: Mine was Filey. So Peter was quite pleased I never asked him to take it.

IAN: Peter Filey? Yes, I can see that. Well today I am feeling so light-hearted I'm up for anything. Let's make up a new surname. How about Freedom? Liberty? Victory?

AUDREY: How about Lucky Escape?

IAN: Perfect. Good morning Vicar, I'm Ian Lucky Escape and this is my wife, Mrs Lucky Escape.

AUDREY: Is that a proposal?

IAN: Of course it is.

Once more they rush into each other's arms. A bottle is kicked out from the back of the couch.

AUDREY: What was that?

IAN: Well, if the SM was sleeping on the couch, it's odds-on the ASM is sleeping behind it.

AUDREY: This is a bit like a Bertie Wooster situation. Perhaps your vicar is hiding behind there too.

IAN: Carlo? Arise and face the music.

One arm climbs onto the back of the couch, then another. Finally, PETER emerges.

Act III – Scene 1

PETER: So you have finally arrived? We've been waiting for you for hours. *[To Audrey.]* Good morning, darling.

AUDREY: My God, Peter. What the hell is going on?

IAN: How long have you been there?

PETER: Well, how long is it since the show finished?

AUDREY: That's rubbish. We were here when the show finished. We waited for ages, then we went to Leo's, and several other places all over town, until finally we came back here because this was the last place we expected to find you – at least before seven this evening.

PETER: Well, you can't have waited long because, somehow, we only got five curtain calls last night.

IAN: *[Loudly]* That's nonsense. You gave us the slip!

PETER: Good morning Ian. Lovely to see you. Would you mind keeping it down? Some of us are trying to sleep.

AUDREY: Get up you idiot and tell us what's going on.

PETER stands up and his pants fall down, revealing that he is wearing a pair of tennis themed undies containing the words 'Big Serve' thereon. He soon pulls up his pants, adjusts his belt and slumps into the couch as IAN and AUDREY stand either side of him downstage.

PETER: We didn't give you the slip. As we were coming offstage one of the tech boys said he had a bottle handy. So we stopped off for a few and got waylaid. We can't have been more than half an hour.

IAN: You must have been at least an hour because we waited that long before we decided to try to find you at Leo's. Why didn't you just come on there as we planned?

PETER: Yeah, we'll I've never really been a spaghetti fan.

AUDREY: Shut up, Peter. I've had a gutful of this type of thing.

PETER: Sorry. Are you sure it wasn't the lasagne at Leo's?

IAN: Where the hell is Joan?

PETER: I have absolutely no idea. I lost track of her once the flagon of Dr Lindeman claret was produced.

IAN: Well, is she all right?

PETER: I'm sure she's fine. She's probably around here somewhere.

IAN rushes at him.

IAN: You bastard.

AUDREY: Ian!

Act III – Scene 1

IAN stops himself and retreats.

IAN: I'm sorry.

PETER: No. Don't apologise. That was no lady; that was your wife.

AUDREY: Peter, stop it.

PETER: I'm sorry. I'm just trying to think. She was around here somewhere.

As he says this we can see one arm then another emerging from behind the couch and JOAN pops up.

JOAN: Morning all!

PETER: Good morning, Love. I knew you were about.

JOAN: Yes. But where that is exactly, I'm not quite sure.

PETER: Don't fear, my love, you are amongst friends.

JOAN: Good.

She gets up and we see that her shirt is unbuttoned and her pants are nowhere near up.

IAN: Good God!

AUDREY: Joan! For Heaven's sake.

JOAN realises what is happening.

JOAN: Ah. You find me in, what Katharine Hepburn once described as "a relative state of undress". Whose pants are these?

PETER: Act two, scene four I think?

She buttons up and joins PETER on the couch.

JOAN: Oh well. Plenty of time to get them pressed and ready for Barry to do his bit with the tuba and the school kid's lunchbox. Ian, be a darling and get me a coffee.

IAN: What?

AUDREY: Have you two been ... doing it?

PETER: Doing what, exactly?

AUDREY: You know ... it.

PETER: Darling, I have no idea what you are talking about. It's far too early for word games.

IAN: If you had ever attended a little thing well known to most people as a 'high school' you would know 'it' is a metaphor.

PETER: Well, I have never, ever done anything as disgusting as a metaphor, nor indeed anything so vulgar as attending a high school.

AUDREY: Stop trying to make a joke out of it all.

Act III – Scene 1

PETER: Well what do you suggest I do?

IAN: Tell us what happened last night.

JOAN: Isn't it obvious? Darlings, there wasn't anything nasty or vicious about it we just got boozing and things, sort of, fell apart from there.

AUDREY: Yes, but ...

JOAN: But what, Audrey?

AUDREY: Have you two been having sex?

PETER and JOAN look at each other for a long time. Then back at IAN and AUDREY.

JOAN: I don't know.

PETER: Yes. What exactly is your definition of sex?

AUDREY: Oh my God!

IAN: People usually know when they have and when they haven't.

PETER: But that is just it, you see. Do they?

JOAN: Yes. Before you came on the scene, Audrey, Peter once told me that he had sex with almost all the members of the chorus line at the Tivoli, but under close questioning none of them seemed to quite agree that it had actually happened.

PETER: So, how do you explain that?

IAN: Did you, or did you not have sexual intercourse with my wife?

PETER and JOAN look at each other again.

PETER: I don't know. Maybe? *[Pause to say something flippant.]* Then again, I'm not a hundred percent sure what you mean. You see, Ian, as you indicated I never really got beyond form one and at my school, which was also pretty rough it must be admitted, we never called 'it' anything like 'sexual intercourse'. There was lots of 'sucking' and 'licking' ...

JOAN: Or 'blowing'!

PETER: Or 'blowing', yes indeed, or 'screwing', 'boning' or 'shagging', but we pretty much subsumed the whole operation under the heading of 'fucking'.

JOAN: Or 'rooting'?

PETER: Sort of. Although that was rather more Moonee Ponds than Essendon.

JOAN: Yes, you lot in Essendon were always rather more refined than us in the Ponds Institute. No doubt the inevitable consequence of all that Presbyterianism.

PETER: No doubt.

AUDREY: You two are completely vulgar.

Act III – Scene 1

JOAN: Surely not completely?

PETER: You wouldn't say, moderately?

IAN: Yes, I think we've had enough of all this. To put it in simple terms that even you can understand, Peter, did you fuck her?

PETER and JOAN look at each other again.

PETER: Possibly.

AUDREY: Peter, you bastard.

PETER: Why are you so upset about it? I don't really know what happened. I might have had intimate relations with half the crew, the chorus line and every member of the box office and front of house staff, for all I know. But what should be perfectly obvious about the whole thing, from the state of my head this morning, is that I had absolutely no intention nor premeditation to do any of it. *[Looks to JOAN.]* Or is it 'do any of them'? *[To IAN.]* You went to high school, Ian, you'll know.

JOAN: It's 'them' I think.

PETER: Really? 'Do any of them.' Doesn't sound right.

AUDREY: That is no excuse, for either of you.

JOAN: I don't see why not. *[She gets up and moves to the dressing table, taking her make-up off and not noticing AUDREY'S note.]* Being plastered

	would certainly get us off both murder and dangerous driving. I fail to see why it shouldn't excuse this minor infraction.

IAN: Minor infraction?

JOAN: Surely you're not upset by a bit of nonsense we might have got up to while under the influence?

AUDREY: A bit of nonsense? I think I'm going mad.

JOAN: Oh come on, you two. We're not twenty-one anymore. Do you think after all we've been through, all of us together, all these years in this theatre and on the road, Peter and I are going to suddenly take up and fall madly in love with each other and only really discover it after a bottle of scotch with the crew, three bottles of champagne with the backers...

PETER: And a flagon of Dr Lindeman claret!

JOAN: It's absurd. I don't care what we did last night. And when you think about it honestly, neither do you. I am sorry if we did, because it was a stupid and irresponsible thing to do. But if we did, it didn't mean a thing and it's particularly silly to go on about it, especially... because it wouldn't have been the first time.

AUDREY: What?

IAN: The first time what?

JOAN: The first time we did 'it'.

Act III – Scene 1

PETER: Ah Joan, perhaps it's not quite the moment.

JOAN: Why not? I've had enough of all this. This isn't a confession. Good Lord, we've been rolling around on each other, and mauling each other on stage almost every night for the last twenty years. Does anyone really think we never did a bit of harmless bonking? It would be sick if we hadn't. And don't look so hurt, Ian. For Goodness sake, it's not love. When we in, what is laughingly referred to as, 'the profession' occasionally give into our bodies and those forces that we can't really cope with, it's not called 'romance', it's called 'rehearsal'. And like most bloody rehearsals it's usually bland, boring, full of mistakes, lacking in motivation and, in relation to anything approximating the search for truth and beauty, totally inadequate. After putting up with us for most of that time and seeing everything about this business that we have all had to endure together, I thought you knew. No. In fact I know you knew.

IAN: That is the most ridiculous piece of show-folk sophistry I have ever heard.

PETER: I didn't think there was anything particularly sophisticated about it. What she is saying is that it is all quite basic really.

AUDREY: So you are telling us that you have been carrying on for years and that you have never bothered to tell us anything about it.

JOAN:	Only because it doesn't mean anything. And it can hardly be described as 'carrying on'. Sounds like a Sid James movie.

JOAN finds the note from AUDREY, reads it, puts it back on the table and holds back from commenting.

PETER:	She's right. In fact, I can hardly remember any of the times we did it at all.
IAN:	Well that's appalling. You should be ashamed of yourselves.
PETER:	What is it exactly that you are objecting to, Ian? That we had some casual sex when we got a bit boozed, or that we did it and didn't care about it?
AUDREY:	Well, I don't believe Joan would be so indifferent to it all.
JOAN:	Really Audrey. What a nice thing to say. You're right. In a way. Apart from last night, I know exactly when we were together, how it happened and how little I felt about it once it had happened. And so does Peter. He's just not as comfortable with the facts as I am.
IAN:	Well, that just goes to show that it's not all about you and what you feel about it. Perhaps it's not so acceptable in 'the profession' after all?

Act III – Scene 1

AUDREY: Well, I don't care if it is. It's totally unacceptable to me. This is not the way I was taught to behave.

PETER: Well, it's not you behaving, Audrey, it's me. And it's Joan. I'm really sorry you are upset and I will do anything you want me to do to make it better.

JOAN: So will I.

AUDREY: I want you to admit that it was wrong. That what you two have been doing is utterly immoral.

PETER: Yeah. Except that.

AUDREY: There it is then. You obviously don't even care.

IAN: Clearly.

PETER: I never said that, Audrey. And if you are really upset and if thinking about our stupidity has hurt you, of course it's wrong. But I don't think it's immoral. I'm not sure anything short of killing someone is really immoral. Shocking, upsetting and maybe even deceitful, but hardly immoral.

IAN: That is a pretty absolute definition of morality, and one that's pretty kind on you, Peter.

JOAN: Look, let's just be absolutely clear about what we are dealing with here.

IAN: I think that is a very good idea.

JOAN:	Five or six times over the last twenty years Peter and I have occasionally fallen into bed for incredibly trivial and pathetic reasons. There have never been any consequences to it, either for our marriages or our business relationship. We are one hundred percent committed to each other as business partners and totally committed to each other's well-being for business and, dare I say it, 'artistic' reasons. In traditional terms, we are not in love. Don't worry. We don't really care for each other's lives outside the business. The day one of us loses her voice or gets a zimmer frame, it's over. We'll visit each other in the nursing home a couple of times a year, send each other the odd Christmas card and make frequent pathetic and misguided attempts at a comeback. But none if it will amount to anything less or more than show business. Am I right, Peter?
PETER:	Sounds right to me. And there is absolutely no business like it!
JOAN:	So where does that leave us four?
IAN:	Well, I think you are both total shits, but I can't think at the moment what is best.
AUDREY:	I don't know. This is such a betrayal of us both. Do you two have any idea what we have had to put up with all these years? All the sacrifices we've made for you and your careers? And now you pay us back like this. I can't accept any of this. I want a divorce, Peter, and I advise you two to do the same.

Act III – Scene 1

PETER: Hang on, Audrey. You're right. I know you've had to put up with a great deal over the years, but I think we need to think very carefully before we start talking about divorce.

AUDREY: Well, I have been thinking very carefully about it for a long time already and that's what I want.

JOAN: Audrey? What's this note about?

PETER: What note?

JOAN: This one.

She holds it up. PETER grabs the note from her.

PETER: "Dear Peter and Joan, we've left to catch the 11.30 from Spencer Street heading for the rest of our lives in the peace and quiet of an undisclosed location to which you are neither invited nor welcome. Ian and Audrey exit stage right, fade lights, the end."

IAN: That's actually pretty good.

PETER: *[Genuinely bemused]* You mean you two are in...

JOAN: 'Love' I think is the shockingly immoral word you are looking for, Peter. I don't think they got up to that by form one at Essendon State School.

AUDREY: Well, what about it? We are in love, as a matter of fact, and it's a very noble profession.

PETER: How can you be?

JOAN: Peter, I think we need to approach this rationally. Audrey, are you saying that you and Ian are...

IAN: Yes, Joan, we are...

JOAN: Please don't, Ian, the adults are talking. Audrey, are you saying that...

AUDREY: Yes, and for some time.

PETER: Oh really. So we are not the only ones indulging in the pleasure of your 'sexual intercourse'?

AUDREY: Yes, in fact, you are. We wanted to wait until we told you.

JOAN: Really? I can't believe that.

IAN: Well, sort of...

AUDREY: No sex at all.

IAN: Yes, that's right. No sex at all.

JOAN: That is disgusting. You two have been in love all this time, not doing anything about it, and now you want to walk out the door together. It's appalling. How can you be so brazen about it? Didn't you think we at least deserve some discussion about it or an explanation?

IAN: That's what last night was supposed to be about.

Act III – Scene 1

PETER: What, you were proposing to take us to Leo's to tell us you were leaving? I doubt it. That's far more Georges' Regency Room and toasted ham sandwiches than Leo's and spaghetti.

AUDREY: Look Peter, we don't have anything to feel guilty about. You two have been carrying on like children for far too long and we're sick of it. We've put up with it for years and clung together for comfort for years too. We never did anything about it because it would have muddied the issue. But now our consciences are clean. We're in the right here and you are in the wrong.

JOAN: This is really the absolute end. Peter and I have occasionally, and usually drunkenly, fallen into bed three seconds before falling asleep, while you two have been nursing a secret, burning, passionate and unconsummated love for twenty years – and now you are claiming the moral high ground?

AUDREY: It hasn't been twenty years.

IAN: Yes, nothing like that.

PETER: Well, how long has it been?

IAN: Much more like ten.

AUDREY: Ten? Are you mad? We couldn't have possibly held onto a secret, burning, passionate and unconsummated love for ten years.

IAN: Speak for yourself.

AUDREY: Now you are being ridiculous.

IAN: Oh really?

AUDREY: Yes. Anyway it's none of their business how long and how passionately we have been holding onto anything?

PETER: Well, I think it is our business. Ian's making a very good point.

IAN: Thanks.

PETER: Any time.

AUDREY: Peter, mind your own business.

PETER: Do you think it's more like eight or nine, Audrey?

IAN: Sounds about right to me.

PETER: Or five or six?

AUDREY: Ian!

JOAN: Well Audrey. I'm sure we'd all like to know.

AUDREY: *[Exasperated]* Well, if you must know, it's probably more like four or five.

JOAN: What? You've been in love since the sixties? I find that very hard to believe.

AUDREY: Why?

Act III – Scene 1

JOAN: Because everyone knows that since flower power falling in love with anyone has been strictly off limits.

PETER: Yes, you are supposed to be in love with everyone.

IAN: Joan, I don't see how you can be such a hypocrite. Sex is far more immoral than love, and you know it.

PETER: She does not. I really don't know how you can say that.

JOAN: He's right. Love is far more immoral than sex. What we've been doing is just playacting. What you've not been doing is the real thing.

AUDREY: That's right. And I don't really care about what you've been doing, when I think about it. I doubt you even know. I just want to get on with the rest of my life. And that means Ian.

PETER: Surely it can't be as definitive as that?

AUDREY: I'm sorry, but it is.

IAN: I feel the same way. In any case there's no use going on about it now. There's not much more we can say for the moment. Audrey, I think we should leave.

JOAN: Yes, I think you should. And you can take your sordid little love romance with you.

IAN: We'll have to talk soon. Perhaps we can think about it for a week or so, then meet and sort everything out.

PETER: Is this all really necessary?

AUDREY: I'm afraid so.

AUDREY and IAN leave. PETER and JOAN slump into the couch, sad, speechless and bemused. As they think about what has happened they get the uneasy feeling that, beyond their business relationship, they don't really know each other at all.

PETER: I am absolutely stunned.

JOAN: Well, I certainly never saw that coming. Do you think they are telling the truth? Or did they just make it up last night to annoy us when we didn't show up?

PETER: It's a pretty elaborate scenario if they did.

JOAN: They certainly didn't take all our bonking in the spirit in which it was intended.

PETER: Extraordinary. Do you really think they were upset by all that or was it just the excuse they have been looking for?

JOAN: They seemed pretty upset.

Act III – Scene 1

PETER: Well, frankly I thought they knew. 'At the job on the job' is practically Living with Showfolk 101. I'm sure they teach a course in it at that university thing they all go to.

JOAN: Heavens. If I thought they were worried about that I would have knocked it off years ago. It was hardly worth all the fuss.

PETER: Thanks very much. Anyway, as I remember, that first time was your idea. You came up with some rubbish about it being important for our development as 'artists of the theatre'.

JOAN: Yes, well you didn't take much convincing.

PETER: What was it then? Pre-show nerves while Ian was away for a few weeks?

JOAN: Something like that, obviously.

PETER: God that was awful.

JOAN: Absolutely hideous. Certainly it was the last time we did it sober?

PETER: Undoubtedly. Anyway, it was hardly the basis of a grand passion. Was it?

JOAN: Not really.

PETER: Hang on. What do you mean by "not really"?

JOAN: *[Quickly]* I mean no.

PETER: That's a relief. For a moment then I thought the world was really turning upside down.

JOAN: Do you know, I think you are much more convincing as a lover when we are doing it on stage.

PETER: *[Really touched]* That's really very kind of you to say so.

JOAN: No, I mean it.

PETER: I know you do. In fact, do you know, I feel the same about you. Don't take this the wrong way, but as soon as we get offstage I can't really see the point of you.

JOAN: Exactly. I don't really want you so much as I just expect you to be there on your cue. That's why I like Ian so much. I really look forward to seeing him and I am really... well, you know, attracted to him.

PETER: Exactly. I feel the same about Audrey. *[Pause.]* Do you know I never realised that people carried on like that outside marriage. That is until this morning. All that love business.

JOAN: It's shocking. Now I'm worried. If people can fall in love outside marriage and hold off on the sex bit, it's the end of civilisation.

PETER: Don't worry. Once they finally get forced into the sex thing they are bound to be back. You can't have both at once. I'd give it the long weekend though.

JOAN: Do you really think so?

PETER: No doubt whatsoever.

Act III – Scene 1

JOAN: I hope you're right. I'm suddenly feeling somewhat uncertain about almost everything at the moment.

PETER: Yes. I know exactly what you mean.

JOAN shows her concern and her gaze meets PETER's look of confidence, which is instantly shattered and now he too is worried.

Lights fade.

Curtain.

www.ingramcontent.com/pod-product-compliance
Lightning Source LLC
Chambersburg PA
CBHW071319080526
44587CB00018B/3279